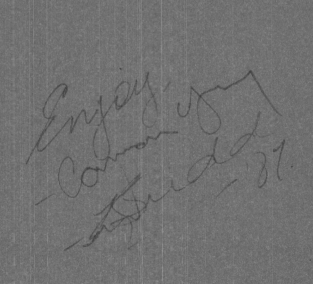

Published in Canada by:

SummerWild Productions Ltd.,
#2202 1275 Pacific Street,
Vancouver, British Columbia V6E 1T6
Ph (604) 681 - 0015

Distributed by:

Whitecap Books Ltd.,
1086 West 3rd Street,
North Vancouver, B.C. V7P 3J6
Ph (604) 980 - 9852

CANADIAN CATALOGUING IN PUBLICATION DATA

Young, Cameron, 1958 -
 Calgary, cowboys and Kananaskis Country

ISBN 0 - 9692807 - 0 - X

1. Calgary Region (Alta.) - Description and travel - Views. 2. Kananaskis Country Provincial Park (Alta.) - Description - Views. I. Budd, Ken, 1942 - II. Title.

FC3697.37.Y69 1987   971.23'3   C87 - 090054 - 4
F1079.5.C35Y69 1987

Designed by Alex Green, Ken Budd
 and Cameron Young

Color separated , printed and bound in Canada by
 D.W. Friesen & Sons Ltd.,
 Altona, Manitoba

# CALGARY
## Cowboys &
## Kananaskis Country

*Photography*
CAMERON YOUNG

*Text*
KEN BUDD

*Foreword*
PETER LOUGHEED

*Graphic Art Direction*
ALEX GREEN

# CALGARY
## Cowboys &
## Kananaskis Country

CAMERON YOUNG

KEN BUDD

Photographed exclusively with

**OLYMPUS OM**
SYSTEM

*cameras & accessories*
*from* W. CARSEN CO. LTD.

Co-produced by

and

# WHITECAP BOOKS
### VANCOUVER/TORONTO

# ACKNOWLEDGEMENTS

It is only appropriate to show appreciation to the many who unselfishly assisted us. So to those named here, we offer a public, yet most personal "THANK YOU!"

* Peter Lougheed

* Alex Green and John Scott

* Sherry and Charlie Ewing

* Robert Chalmers and the Cowboys of the Sheep Creek Round-Up

* Al Greenough and the C — N Branding Crew

* Dale Jacobson and Neil Clark of the Brooks Wildlife Centre

* Brian Keating and Trish Exton of the Calgary Zoo

* Cam Innes and the Calgary Stampeders

* Mark Stevens and the Calgary Cannons

* Rick Skaggs and the Calgary Flames

* Grace and Chris Hamilton of Zero Copy Ltd.

* Les Richards for technical assistance

* Elaine Jones for editing assistance

* The Staff of Whitecap Books

* The Staff of Nova Photo

* Jean Gelwicks, Steve Macdonald and Angie Chan

* Don and Rod Miller-Tait

* Harvey and Ginger Young

* Pat Welch

* David Friesen and D.W. Friesen & Sons Ltd., and,

* Michael Burch (never the last, nor the least!)

# DEDICATIONS
*To my family—*MOM, DAD, SCOTT, SUSAN *and* MAGGIE.

*To* 'THE BROMLEY CLAN',
*my surrogate family,*
TOM, SCOTT, JASON *and* CLAY,
*my exceptional nephews,*
*and,*
JEFF,
*again, in appreciation.*

# TABLE OF CONTENTS

*"This publication is a fitting tribute to three themes that are very close to me—the impressive City of Calgary, my home; the cowboy, that unique individual whose lifestyle has colorfully enhanced my own life; and, Kananaskis Country, a mountain paradise I feel proud to have helped create."*

PETER LOUGHEED

# INTRODUCTION

The first bond between 'CALGARY, Cowboys & Kananaskis Country' is their regional proximity. Calgary spreads from the banks of the Bow and Elbow rivers, midway between the borders of British Columbia and Saskatchewan, and in the lower quarter of the province of Alberta. On ranches and in small communities around this major centre resides the cowboy. In Calgary's backyard, and on the cowboy's backstep, is Kananaskis Country, a newly developed park and an eternally beautiful mountain splendor.

But proximity isn't the only link between these three themes.

There is also a shared history.

The Kananaskis Valley was one of the transportation corridors used by the early pioneers while utilizing routes to the west through the Palliser, the Rogers and the Crowsnest passes. The first cowboys came from that hardy stock of pioneers. Calgary was not only a stopover for those enroute to the west, but also a special place for cowboys of the region to visit.

And it is people and their lifestyles.

Many Calgarians are keen outdoor types, as are cowboys by nature of their work. When looking for a place to enjoy the outdoors, the adventuresome choose Kananaskis Country. Cowboys spend time there too. They herd cattle into this area during the spring, and leave them to graze there over the summer. In the fall, there is the traditional round-up and cattle drive home.

Mostly it is an attitude.

Calgarians love their city. They love its western flavor, its youthful, growing energy. They are also very partial to the country to the west, where within a short drive they are in a scenic wonderland. The cowboy's lifestyle parallels that strong attachment. It symbolizes the essence of what it means to be a 'westerner', and to value the spirit of rugged individualism, so well represented by the untamed wilderness of Kananaskis Country.

There are many words that could compare and characterize these subjects. Vitality, charisma and spirit are just a few. Whichever are chosen, they can all be used interchangeably with Calgary, cowboys or Kananaskis Country.

*Budd*

# CALGARY

To the east, grasshopper songs rise from the flat prairie in the shimmering heat. To the north and south, in wooded hollows between hillocks, deer ignore the blazing sun and browse in the shade. And to the west, a hawk soars amidst jagged, snow-capped peaks that challenge the heat.

At the hub of this varied topography, gleaming skyscrapers penetrate the vast blue. Like a playful colt not yet ready to assume its final form, Calgary stretches its lengthening muscles.

It began over a century ago as a fort built by the North West Mounted Police to provide order for the lawless frontier. As the buffalo hide trade declined, it was recognized that the open range surrounding the tiny settlement was conducive to ranching. Concessions allowing long term leases on large parcels of land, and the arrival of the 'Iron Horse' ensured ranching would be a mainstay of the area.

A hundred years later and a metropolis burgeons where buffalo roamed. Oil derricks are responsible for the glass towers that reflect the city's prosperity. Almost three-quarters of a million people spill from the banks of the Bow and Elbow rivers into the prairie and the foothills.

Dozens of locations within the city provide opportunities for enjoyment. The meandering Bow River is the scene of picnics in parks that border its banks. The Zoo entices young and old to investigate intriguing displays. Heritage Park personifies yesteryear - an entire, turn-of-the-century village, authentically recreated.

Every summer the city reverberates with echoes of this heritage as the spectacular Calgary Stampede entertains a million visitors from around the world. Hospitality from the residents is at its finest, and that proverbial good time is had by everybody.

Perhaps the weather contributes to the affable personalities of the citizenry. The semi-arid climate brings hot summers, popular with outdoor enthusiasts. Warm chinook winds offer respites from bitter winters. And constant throughout the seasons is the brilliant sunshine that blesses those who live in this fascinating land of the big sky.

*Squirt wars.* **(Riley Park)**

*Bearers of good tidings.* ('Heidi' & 'Howdy', Stampede Parade)

*Balloons, baubles and bales.* (Nose Hill)

*Electric emeralds.* (Downtown Calgary)

*Summer symphonies in the park.* (Riley Park)

*A traditional display.*

*Fandangos flourish.*

*Keeping the dance alive.*  **(Folk Arts Festival, Prince's Island Park)**

*Sails on ripples of silver.* (Glenmore Reservoir)

*Overcoming the phobia
by petting the python.*
**(The Zoo)**

*For beautiful skin, moisturize daily.* **(The Zoo)**

*"Go ahead and touch,
but no nose jokes!"*
**(The Zoo)**

*"Have you seen those tacky lawn ornaments?"* **(The Zoo)**

*A garden before Eden.*  **(Prehistoric Park, The Zoo)**

*Creatures from another time.*  **(Prehistoric Park, The Zoo)**

29

*The metropolis and its hinterland.* **(Calgary)**

*Urban Tarzans.* **(Elbow River)**

*Skywalk freeway.* **(Downtown Calgary)**

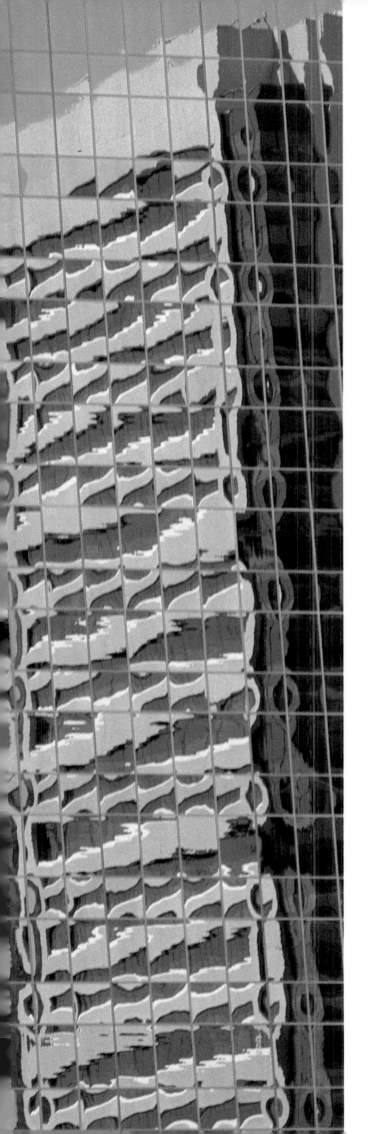

*Shimmering monoliths.* (**Downtown Calgary**)

*Angle power.* (**Downtown Calgary**)

*Outdoor/indoor architecture.*
**(Devonian Gardens)**

*Medieval cowboys.* **(Glenbow Museum)**

*City symbols.* **(Calgary Tower)**

*Indoor/outdoor architecture.*
**(PetroCanada Building)**

*Conversation in bronze.* (Stephens Avenue Mall)

*Reflections of the past.* (City Halls - Old in New)

*'Cannon' power.* (Cannon Baseball, Foothills Stadium)

*Rubber armada.* (Raft Races, Bow River)

*Duelling cycles.* (Glenmore Velodrome)

*Relaxed anticipation.*
(Tour of the Sun Cycle Race
Downtown Calgary)

*Masters of the marathon.* (Calgary Marathon)

A well-deserved rest. (Nose Hill)

*Perfection suspended.* **(Spruce Meadows National)**

*Equestrian combatants.* **(Calgary Polo Club)**

*Living history.* (**Heritage Park**)

*Classics from yesteryear.* (**Heritage Park**)

*A walk back in time.* **(Heritage Park)**

*Paddle power.* **(S.S. Moyie, Heritage Park)**

*Pride in past accomplishments.* **(Heritage Park)**

*'Foothills Express'.* **(Heritage Park)**

*Warm prairie nights.* (The Saddle Dome and Calgary Skyline)

*The annual 'Battle of the Titans'.*  **(Stampeder Football, McMahon Stadium)**

*Bruisers brawl.*

*Veins of gold.*

*Gladiators on ice.* (Calgary Flames Hockey, Saddle Dome)

*A ride with a 'rush'.*

**(The Luge, Canada Olympic Park)**

*Broomball buffoonery.*  **(Winter Festival, Prince's Island Park)**

*Home on the range - hobby style.* **(Coach Hill)**

*Standing tall.*
**(Henry Moore Sculptures,
Calgary School District Centre)**

*A captivating culture.*  (**Stampede Parade**)

*A North West Mountie on parade.*
(**Stampede Parade**)

*Traditional finery.*  (**Stampede Parade**)

*A 'priority' pancake.* **(Pancake Breakfast)**

*Allemande left.* **(Square Dance Demonstration)**

*Aristocratic arrogance.* **(Calgary Stampede)**

*A stetson serenade.* (Calgary Stampede)

*The many faces of the midway.*

**(Calgary Stampede)**

*Chariots of the range.* (Chuckwagon Races, Calgary Stampede)

# Cowboys

A yearling steer breaks from the herd and bounds into the aspen forest beside the trail. An outrider spurs his gelding's flanks and charges into the thicket after the stray.

Silent signals between man and horse - knee pressure, a shift of weight and neck reining - allow them to work as one, weaving in and out of the trees at a dangerous clip. Branches are staved off by a wide-brimmed stetson and slick leather chaps. Circling the obstinate steer, they block its escape and force it back to the herd.

It is a scene that could have taken place a century ago - men and horses driving cattle through wooded, mountain passes, the world ablaze with the color of changing leaves against the crisp blue of the autumn sky.

The 'Cattle Kingdom' that developed in this part of the continent around 1884 gave birth to the traditions of round-ups, roping and branding. It was also responsible for the cowboy - a welcome anachronism in the highly technological world of today.

Cowboys are a rare breed. Defying the laws of reason, the more intrepid of their lot gather at fairgrounds around the continent to demonstrate the mastery they have achieved with the skills of their trade. Nowhere is this better displayed than at the Calgary Stampede. Here they rope calves, bulldog steers and even milk cows. They jar their brawn and their brains aboard wild broncs. They confront danger on its own terms by climbing on top of the pliable hide of a Brahma bull.

All in the name of sport? Perhaps, but there is probably more. It seems to be the way a cowboy celebrates, as well as the manner in which he preserves his identity, his craft and his heritage.

And the cowboy needs to think of preservation. With the advent of huge feedlots, the break-up of large tracts of land, and the automated methods available to ranchers, it will take the kind of resolve and dedication to the lifestyle that has been shown for the last century to keep him from becoming a vanishing breed. It would be everyone's loss if that came to pass.

*Gearing up.* (Calgary Stampede)

*Countdown.* (Bareback Riding, Calgary Stampede)

*Reach for the sky!* (Bareback Riding, Calgary Stampede)

*Standoff.* (Steer Wrestling, Calgary Stampede)

*Blue jeans and stetsons - a cowboy's credentials.* (**Calgary Stampede**)

*Teamwork.*  (**High River Rodeo**)

*Lasso magic.* (**Calf Roping, Calgary Stampede**)

*Strawstacks.* (Calgary Stampede)

*Buckaroo dreamer.*  **(Calgary Stampede)**

*The waiting game.*  **(Calgary Stampede)**

*The ultimate challenge.* (Bull Riding, Calgary Stampede)

*A prairie emblem.  (High River)*

*A cowpoke's coffee break.*  (Sheep Creek Reserve, Long Prairie)

*Drivin' 'em home*  (Sheep Creek Reserve)

*Range rider.* **(Long Prairie)**

*The protégé.* **(High River)**

*'Little dogie'.* **(Sheep Creek Reserve)**

*Lariat wizardry.*  (**Strathmore**)

*Brand names.* (C-N Ranch, Strathmore)

*Cattle country.* (**Jumping Pound Creek**)

*Home from the hills.* **(Porcupine Hills)**

# Kananaskis Country

Mountaintops bloom with the pink of dawn. Deep night shadows lose their battle with light. Pine scent prevails and birdsong picks at the silence.

The long guard hairs on the shoulder hump of the grizzly shine with a honey glow in the early morning rays. The bear lumbers across the high alpine meadow in the direction of its daybed, stopping only to strip more berries from low shrubs or to check the slight breeze with its wet, black snout.

In the valley below, in campgrounds and at the edges of lakes, only man's world disturbs the serenity. Hikers eager to get an early start on the trail and fishermen determined to tempt elusive trout with their lures busy themselves in purposeful activity.

It is this blend of co-existence - man and wild creatures at one with the environment - that is the central focus of this remarkable place. This is Kananaskis Country, a twenty-five-hundred-square-mile mountain paradise, bounded by transportation corridors, a forest reserve, and Banff National Park.

Established in 1977 as a recreational playground, the area comprises two different land forms. The portion to the east is forested foothills interspersed occasionally with rolling, carpeted grasslands. Deer vie with cattle for pasture rights. To the west are majestic peaks, capped with glaciers and pitted with chasms. Dense forests of evergreens climb valley walls, and jewelled lakes form in the basins. Bighorn sheep, black bear, elk, moose and deer are often seen, while mountain goat, cougar and grizzly hide from sight.

This place teems with activities year round. Summertime invites fishing, and golfing the superb Kananaskis course delights even professionals. The more adventuresome challenge cliffs, attack rapids in kayaks, and foray with packs on backs into the more remote wilderness. Blankets of snow entice winter campers. Skiers carve graceful turns down slopes or lazy tracks through meadows. And all the time, all around, some of the most stunning scenes in nature await those who venture into this mountain kingdom.

*Delicate, gentle and graceful.* (Mule Deer, Sheep Creek Trail)

*Invitation to adventure* (Highway #40, Kananaskis Country)

*Warning the colony.*

(**Richardson Ground Squirrel, Ptarmigan Cirque Trail**)

*Golden carpets on green foothills.* (**Cochrane**)

*Top of the world.* (Burstall Pass)

*Little bighorn.* (Rocky Mountain Bighorn Lamb, Gorge Creek)

*Granite geometrics.* (Mt. Brock)

*Pink bristles.* (Indian Paintbrush, Mt. Sarrail)

*White water daredevil.* (Kananaskis River)

*Tranquility.* (Barrier Lake)

*Lace filigree.* (Upper Kananaskis Lake)

*Nature in copperplate.* **(Bragg Creek)**

*A new season, a new look.* (Chester Lake)

*Nature's sculptings.* **(Troll Falls)**

*Après ski lair.* (Mount Allan)

*A world stage.* (Mount Allan)

*Downhill dynamo.* (Nor-Am Race, Mount Allan)

*Camping capers.* **(Porcupine Creek)**

*Mountain mystique.* (Kananaskis Lake)

*A cross-country caravan.* (Elk Pass)

*A putter's paradise.* **(Kananaskis Golf Course)**

*Biding his time.* **(Whiskey Jack, Sibbald Creek)**

*Lots of brawn, little beauty.* (Chester Lake)

*Triumph.* (Fortress Mtn.)

*Burdens discarded.* (Chester Lake)

# ON THE DOORSTEP

The hinterland surrounding Calgary is a mix of diverse topographies, and with these different land forms come equally divergent opportunities. All of them present exceptional experiences to the visitor and resident alike.

To the west, beyond Kananaskis Country, lies Banff National Park. The charming village of Banff offers tourists all the amenities, as well as a prestigious educational complex, The Banff Centre. But the wildness is the main attraction - glaciers, snowfields, waterfalls, awesome peaks and spectacular views.

To the south, sandy foothills give rise to impressive lodgepole pine and spruce forests. This is the Porcupine Hills region, a major centre for ranching. The hills are home to deer, elk, black bear, lynx, cougar, porcupine - and cattle. The eastern slopes are blanketed with rolling grasslands, and along their base sit the communities of High River, Nanton, Stavely, Claresholm and Fort McLeod, service centres for the farmlands that stretch further eastward.

To the east, a carpet of 'prairie wool' - hardy, nutritious grazing pasture - has dominated the plains for eons. It has been the rivers that have brought a different face to the land through a network of irrigation ditches, allowing agriculture to flourish. It has been the rivers too, that have helped expose an elusive quarry buried beneath the clay of the moonscape-like Dinosaur Park Badlands on the Red Deer River near Brooks. Archeologists have found the haunting beauty of this dramatic setting to be a treasure trove in their search for links with man's past.

And to the north are varied landscapes. To the northeast is prairie. To the northwest are lush, forested foothills. Between the two is a blend, an undulating countryside of farms, fences, woodlands and lakes. Summer sun creates an aquatic playground at Sylvan Lake, west of Red Deer, while the cold of winter encourages recreation of another sort. Whatever the season, there is always a glorious sunset to end special days.

*Etching a trail.* (Peyto Glacier, Banff National Park)

*An alpine village.* (Banff Townsite, Banff National Park)

*Palatial lodgings.* (Banff Springs Hotel, Banff)

*The epitome of class. (Lake Louise, Banff National Park*

*Some things never change.* (Porcupine Hills)

*Residue.* (Red Deer River Badlands)

*Quarry on the wing.* (Brooks)

*Travelling through time.* (Dinosaur Provincial Park, Brooks)

*A fitting end.* **(Sylvan Lake)**